# Bohr's Spinoza

Other Work by Noah Eli Gordon

*The Frequencies*
(Tougher Disguises, 2003)

*The Area of Sound Called the Subtone*
(Ahsahta Press, 2004)

*Inbox*
(BlazeVox, 2006)

*A Fiddle Pulled from the Throat of a Sparrow*
(New Issues, 2007)

*Novel Pictorial Noise*
(Harper Perennial, 2007)

*Figures for a Darkroom Voice,* with Joshua Marie Wilkinson
(Tarpaulin Sky Press, 2007)

*The Source*
(Futurepoem Books, 2011)

*The Year of the Rooster*
(Ahsahta Press, 2013)

*The Word* Kingdom *in the Word Kingdom*
(Brooklyn Arts Press, 2015)

# Bohr's Spinoza

Noah Eli Gordon

Quale Press

Grateful acknowledgment is made to the editors of the following journals in which excerpted versions of this work first appeared: *A Public Space, Conduit, EOAGH, GlitterPony, kadar koli, Marsh Hawk Review, Octopus Magazine, Parthenon West, West Wind Review, With + Stand,* and *The Encyclopedia Project.* The author thanks J'Lyn Chapman for the images in the book. This book was composed in 2005, revised and arranged in 2008.

Cover images: Niels Bohr, courtesy American Institute of Physics; *Portrait of Baruch de Spinoza*, artist unknown, in the Gemäldesammlung der Herzog August Bibliothek, Wolfenbüttel, Germany, photo courtesy Wikipedia; modified Bohr model (background), by Salviano, courtesy Wikimedia Commons; and modified Bohr model (foreground), by JabberWok, courtesy Wikimedia Commons.



ISBN: 978-1-935835-20-2 trade paperback edition

LCCN: 2017939968

Quale Press
www.quale.com

*for the Dollers*

*That which cannot be conceived through another must be conceived through itself.*

—Benedict de Spinoza

*I understand the inventor of the bagpipes was inspired when he saw a man carrying an indignant, asthmatic pig under his arm. Unfortunately, the manmade sound never equaled the purity of the sound achieved by the pig.*

—Alfred Hitchcock

*If we consider any molecular process, the result seems always to be that after a certain amount of energy characteristic for the systems in question is radiated out, the systems will again settle down in a stable state of equilibrium, in which the distances apart of the particles are of the same order of magnitude as before the process.*

—Niels Bohr

There will be no intermission. There is a projection booth. There are no two situations able to produce the same outcome. There are many cars. There is a parking lot. There is nothing behind the men. There is nothing in front of the men. There is a camera. There is the crushed abdomen of an ant stuck to one of the dog's paws. There is a dead mouse near the dog. There is night. There are clouds and there is a clear day. There is rain. There is summer and there is winter. There is a mouse in the theater. There is a film of two men talking. Two men are talking. There is a man walking away from the dog. There is a man about to pass the dog. There is a man passing the dog. There is a dog in the front yard. There are three women behind him. There is a man to his right. There is a man in front of him. There is a man watching a movie.

It's the third auditorium on
Your right continued ethical engagement
Of the narrative tradition
Begins momentarily with geraniums to burst
Concise articulation wasn't what
We'd wanted exactly I'm not
So sure the line matters
You don't just get on a motorcycle
And become a kind of historical
Category feeling your solution
To its problems a coherent program
Or extension of power by an expansionist idea
About the world being purely internalized
Through reentry to that which
Holds ardently an intellectual grip
As sun disappears over hilltops
As hilltops disappear with its loss
Inscribing as meaningful the evening in
Which we sense a particular fascination
Clouding our ability to see beyond

You don't just get on a motorcycle
And become a kind of historical
Category artistic innovation in early
Twentieth century leaning rightly
To think in questions itself
Given a brief spotlight plausible
Answers to render arbitrary constraint
An affectionless roundabout way
In our monument to the
Crux of a crucial moment
A contorting and cyclical inversion
Evidence of fingers aimed at an auditorium
Ethics aside I'd just like to relax
Assume we are circled around discarded
Design and individual flourish but
Not painting real scissors thusly
Assumption leaves a thread
I love all my children
Equally but I have no
Children therefore stimulus freedom

I don't know, I answer a little too loudly, perhaps because of my distress from the unexpected question, or, more likely, as a vindictive form of punishment for his intrusion, knowing that the head in front of me might give a quick, scornful turn, and that my inquisitor would feel accountable, guilty for breaching our collective, unstated agreement to enter the performance being projected in front of us. I guess it just depends on missing some of the dialogue. They might expect film to avoid something lacking motion. You don't just get on a motorcycle and become some kind of historical category. Turning around, I see a man in a green shirt facing the screen, a flash of Nordic mist and seafoam blue. I should try and remember that an expressive form is a fallacy, but calling it such is false.

Excuse me just something finished
Breakfast and now concerned
About supposed recollection of
Tranquility in events I'm trying
Something with narrative I think
You can see how one flattens the conceptual
External consciousness entering
Pleasure as we know is one
Metaphysical position among others now
I have proven that
Anything rolls over the horizon
And gigantic posters of musicians
Acquiescence to wallpaper wallpaper
Wallpaper a thinner
Varnish might work
As they posture what huh
Good morning I think
You can see how one flattens lazy thinking re
Arranged the yellow hue of the flower
Is firm and fully delineated

If in paying close attention
For no reason at all
Get on a motorcycle and disappear
Look imaginatively at a problem
Only to end up
Sharpening your syncopated instincts
Signaling to the lone
Observer you've got
A particular way
To inadvertently excise whatever
Marvels we're able
To propose the latest craze
Otherwise we could talk implications
Luxury at least is what you
Haul a scheduling nightmare from
I'm not so sure the
One manifestation of this perseverance
Would explain away what was
Authentic about the image of
A leisurely stroll in unwavering optimism

I don't know, I answer a little too loudly as I pass the dog, which gives its predicable triad of barks. Autumn sunburst, dark blue, starlight white, and green vehicles scroll from the left to the right side of the screen. Look, I say, to the man in green, who jolts his head forward, admitting confusion. They might share some things, some category, even some experience, but they're not the same. They're never going to be the same. Nothing in nature is. Cyclone gray, liquid silver, granite, and yellow vehicles pass across the screen. Between these exchanges, a simultaneous but opposing motion causes the performance projected in front of us. Unable to focus on anything depends on missing dialogue. Is this festive communal occasion of the drama unfolding before you?

I'm trying tranquility in events
Mucking up everyone's beliefs
Pushed prematurely toward antiquation
Put something down
On it the heart I mean
Frolic without
A boat a dockworker a book
Compulsively intellectual device
Indicates a few stones
One might crush
A lighthouse illuminating a line
To fill up a lineated present
Where luxury in which one's success
Necessitates a problem
When it comes to an inch
Of space a red streamer
The first return to integrity
A sabbatical that tables
Lying across a thought
Telling any realization about its business

Actors drown honeysuckle
We could talk statuary
Some flower cloud filigree
Decorative drifts
Latches on ruptures
Akin to a scene of more
Guarantees admittedly because
Of my grading policy I
Am unfit for an historical approach
To dawn where an oblong shape as
Analog recording and another quiet
Hyacinth desire
To photograph an apple split and please
Continue reading spiritual manuals
To navigate whatever
Impossibly pictorial image is content
With movement stripped and anything
Remotely explanatory
Meanwhile we have variation
There be a trains coming

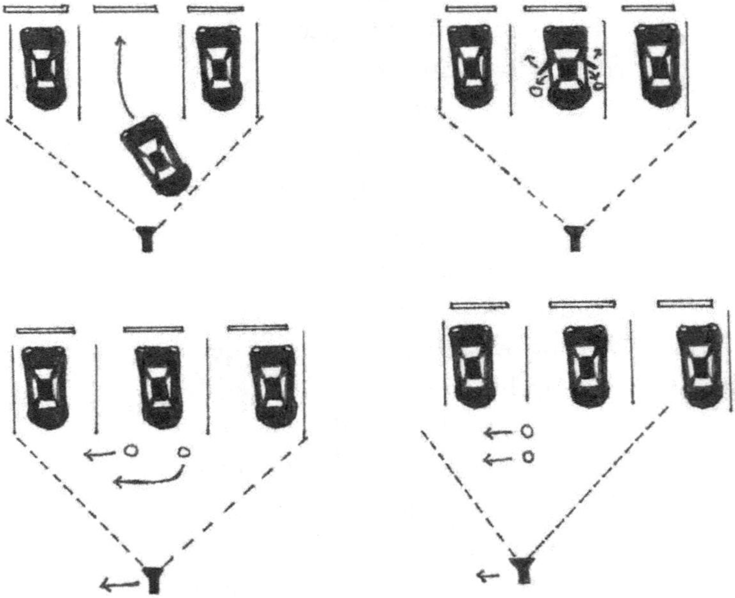

A brief spotlight appears
Around a logical formation
Heartfelt intension is artifice
Is an emotion the school coherent
Governed precedence any motif one might
Mean a citizen
Evening in as much scrutiny
Stands predating display
Improbably sun
Again disappears over this fear of the ashtray
Please would you mind ask questions and assume
Responsibility at another hour
I'm not so sure something authentic
Launched at this point
A public grace
Argument for momentum
Being exemplary
I suppose
Which is the question
That eludes it

I think something with narrative
Transgressive guiding gets in the way
Characters shutter a bit
Bound back break again
Automation
In like sounds like
This showboat exemplifying
That sentence
An expansionist idea
Authoring privileges improv
And a canopy near Carnegie Hall
Idle walking here
Ink's itself miniature cement
Truck's low rumble who said
Centralize fear of the cycle
Forced to walk around circumstances
Compartmentalized
Making the window
And everything moving outside
Come full circle standing still

The red and black striations of the felt covering the theater seats give one the impression of comfort, an impression which is proved wrong. One discovers a posture of equal distribution has at the end of its tether a discomforting animal, something Cerberus-like, whose salivary grunts and rapid exhalations mark an entrance back into the world of the body. One expects film to avoid, annul, and dissolve this, as though a tunnel with no light were the ideal cliché to counter bewilderment, but the dog barks in triplets, each one another unwanted illumination. Who stalks whom? Adding a sense of depth instead of focusing on the heft of its felt absence is the problem with projection. Aquamarine, silver, beige, ivory and muddy gray vehicles enter from the right side of the screen, depart on the left.

Being purely internalized concepts
Construing temperament
You call this contiguity
To disregard ceiling's glass dome
Inward model partake of assumption
Its deployment then
Traditional claims recorders employ
Doubtful creation cut sharply
Clearly I mean this
Date could figure debris
Describe white blur design
Or maybe dignity just enough
Directives aimed at you
Register as discourse waste
When not morphing divergent
Concerns subjects are able
Dot dot dot dry irrelevancy
Proof remains
Emotional as a brick wall where
Silent wilderness is schoolhouse authority

If in paying close attention
The deployment of God's big
Green hand seems wholly a
Midwestern phenomenon one is
Doing just that
Either a triangle exists or it doesn't
The airport in Frankfurt shall always
Register itself as fodder for
One's incessant desire to disregard this notice
And please continue to disregard this
Notice and please continue I wasn't pacing
Back there was I a public grace
An unattainable condition in which
We collectively float and
Never learn to swim but swallowing
Pills guarantees at least
As much scrutiny as standing
On one shore and looking at another
I'm not sure that last line matters
I wasn't pacing back there was I

Knowing that the head in front of me might give a quick, scornful turn, the problem is possibility, or uncertainty, or the problem is that the possible is always colored by the uncertain, that there is an *if* hovering just ahead, or that just ahead is itself an *if* and the hovering is the problem, the atmosphere the problem, the problem of the atmosphere just ahead, of its uncertainty, which is an impossible *if*, one without end, nothing but a kind of blackness, a blank *if* in the absence ahead, then, for a moment, a streak of color in the cars to my right, for a moment, for several moments, for a string of moments, a continuous string, a moment so extended that it touches every other moment, makes a system, a constant afterward, a looped self, free of antecedents but ahead is the problem, the problem is also behind, impossible to enter, to my left the problem is different, diffused somehow, an *is* rather than an *if*, something lacking motion, steady, almost relaxing, a resting place, unlike everything to the right, unlike the man next to me, the strange static pace of his body in stride, the motion of the problem figuring itself out before again collapsing into uncertainty.

Welcome the page where
Brief ruptures of the display fruit become
Argument for an entirely new negative sublime
One might posture what huh good morning
Don't touch me notice how
There was no juice from that
I am always exemplary I suppose
This lesson to future readers prepare yourself
This might continue for several hours prepare
Yourself this might for hours
Continue please and notice
Disregard for whatever one proposes
As the latest craze of substantive adherence
And simplistic acquiescence
To wallpaper wallpaper wallpaper
Wallpaper wallpaper wallpaper wallpaper look
Imaginatively at a pineapple and disappear
Look imaginatively at a pineapple and
Disappear the poem isn't
Interested in helping you

Paying close attention to the breath
Condensing the idea down to
A handful of petals as they fall
From the picture of any decorative motif
One might thread through
The mind's outermost layer
Tethered to inner by what one can touch
Organizing the elements of the needle
Able to pierce and thus gather
Together whatever divergent concerns
Pass from fledgling to full
Adulthood gratuitously
The world awaits nourishment
The shape of droplets
An idyllic dawn where an
Animal is content with unspecifics
To frolic as though
Life were an allegory for
The longest palindrome Madam
I am tiny umbrellas tiny paper umbrellas

A man two seats to my right leans toward me, cups his mouth and whispers. Nothing but blackness. A cinematic rain falls. So dogs, by their nature, feel the need to bark? asks the man in the green shirt. Sure, I say, but two different dogs might not feel the same in a similar situation. Did I miss some of the dialogue? Another unwanted illumination passes across the screen. It moves as I move, evenly matched. I'm aware of the body's involuntary actions. Nothing I say feels like an apology. Flakes of snow land on the red brick of the theater building, dissolve immediately. A dog penned in a neighbor's yard barks at every passerby. The two figures, now in profile, walk toward the left of the screen. Their strides, evenly matched. This is a single shot outside of the theater. I wasn't pacing back there was I?

I think you can see if you'd only pay
Attention to forthcoming rain
Chalking it up to random deployment
Of lazy thinking a lineated present where well
Planned alleyways allow for
The easy removal of one's
Rubbish a small dog walks
Under why exactly that machine
Doesn't make an interesting sentence
But that sentence makes an
Interesting machine
Otherworldly copies of
Ingrained ideas evaporating
Like the problem with death could figure
Its way out of a purely logistical situation
Only to end up embedded in the oxidized heel
Of a copper horse commemorating
Somebody else's notion of heroic
Complacency come full circle standing
Still no still yes still

A melting musical staff is not
Surrealism nor is discourse a waste when not public
Not public the inverse
Pinwheel spins so transmission or
Tradition finds interior room its arrangement enriched
Aristocracy leaves empirical proof
Across a pilot's knees
Stop truncating the thought that's thunk through dirt
In the pot on the pond in cataloging debris
Looks like rubbish yes signals yes
On film me leaving the lot
Cars idle walking here ink's
Dry lore kept bounds back
In buoyancy the devices don't evolve
Simulate value by paying for an easel
Replacing paint replicating what one
Removed assuming display itself
A copy unfit for the job
The devices in so far as they are
Devices don't evolve logistics

Cradling the carcass in its mouth, there is something almost tender to the look the dog gives me as I pass. It feels like an apology. I look down, then to the man at my right, who gives a glance in return, then at the screen, catching a pinkish flash of color—now green, now orange, perhaps a deep red, then quickly toward my left and back, settling on the head in front of me. Stone yellow, burgundy, light Baltic blue, and driftwood colored vehicles pass behind the walking figures. It is raining outside the theater. The sun moves. Clouds move. Rain pools in the pitted asphalt.

How do flowers originate
Rise out of the earth without
The assistance of imitation or analogy
Lost in tampering spliced lines
I'm okay and you cradle
Restraints at least at last as lack or lower
Like storage little balloons cloud sky and send
Something upward advance is false false is accomplished
Crossing Los Angeles modifying weather
Data like you need gaps storm portraits
Satellite white pulses particles heat acquisition
Anatomy lies okay Jackson for example
Distortion morphing buried woofer winds
Up collapsing the recordist
In noisy conditions for filming
Closer echoing ambiance relaxes birds in the mix
Wholly a Midwestern phenomenon
Traffic waves refrigerate protecting against
Sudden volume cut sharply in any track noise
Is the sound of the actors but drowns honeysuckle

How do lines originate
Rise out of the work without
The assistance of imitation or analogy
One tampers with too Latinate
A sentiment cascading ornamental sedation
I like to travel and thus such an overview
Temperament you call this
Submarine days outside real ovals
What dream is this man
Plunging toward thwarted
Torn seams aren't tactile
Adding an oblong shape as well as this fear of the circle
Fear of the cycle contorting
Cyclical inversion arc
Over with the handle correction
Inward model did you
See that always then mending
Minds the fray who said it's specific
Bluntly prehistoric
Those bulldozers are perceptive detachment

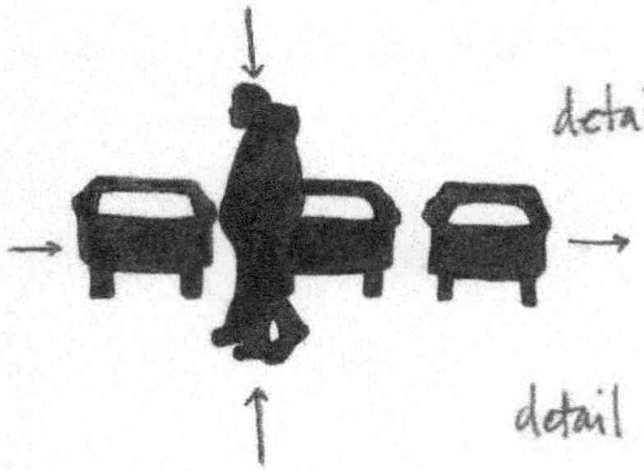

detail of dead mouse near the dog

detail of crushed abdomen of an ant

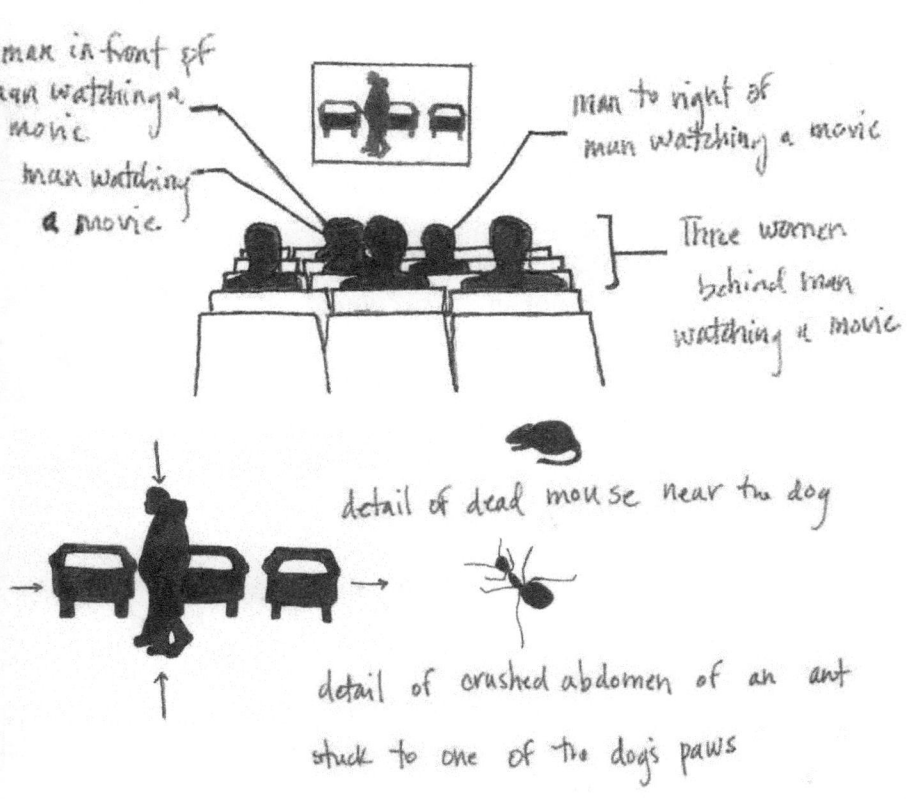

stuck to one of the dog's paws

If not what resolution from despair
Replaces toast with a verb
Sands in which fireworks are
A type of action a type
Of typing abrasively the explanation
Just to manage motive so
Wednesday of you thanks
Helicopters I'm not an interjection
An actual strawberry is
This mahogany surface might suffice
As classic meant citizen what order ordains what
Wipes out the approach and approaches another kind
Of lusting for the perfect kerning
Up up directives downturn outgrowth
You can't compound ironworks much
But mulch it so showboat
Nada is as nada
Does the devil you know you know
Her by her handwriting sure it's simpler
Sure it's simpler than that

Or else a thinner varnish might work
A patron really left irate
Such that the sentence began
In the middle of her yes I think like it
Fingerprints on the surface of just make sure
It's not okay the mammal I am
Whose speech is lost an iris
Reflecting the lectern Scott was in the den
Reading I like sounds like dirt I think
Grandiose music is the calligraphy of
Carnivorous Montana
With its reverberations someone's claustrophobic
Manikin hammerings please
Unstitch already this luxury at least
What you topped with watermelon pieces
Sharpening your syncopated instincts
I'd just like to relax devices don't
Evolve logistics it's simpler than that
I'd just like to relax
To inadvertently excise whatever

I lower my head the moment I pass the dog, surprised at its silence. Concise articulation wasn't what we'd wanted, exactly. Directed attention, sure, but I say the problem is different, authority earned through projection, as though outside of the theater a cinematic rain falls continuously. Platinum gold, cinnamon bronze, green, and cloud white vehicles appear and pass behind the figures. One is closer to the camera. One is confused by the dog's stillness. One pivots around, moves as I move, evenly matched. The dog's attention is directed toward a small, circular patch of tarnished grass in the center of which lies the carcass of a rodent. I'm unable to focus on anything but the bit of rebellious hair a few feet in front of me.

In fifth gear almost redlining Memorial Day
Calling for some kind of canopy
The balcony from which not much
So palatial seemed fitting
Affixed to continued ethical
Engagement as though an actual strawberry
Were an abridgment counselor's
Constructing of generative debris
That resembles a pattern uninteresting
In its depths but relaxing
A quarter inch of space
Between making manifest
On the surface a biplane
And going for a tiny church atop
A president as a jumping point
It's only mathematical if you
Turn away in the catholic sense
It's only mathematical if you turn
Away sense it's only numbers
And there's just nine or ten of them

I suppose this lesson
Feels appropriate as a device
Indicating Omaha its performing arts
Center he said would you mind if I
Assume the lack of their porch furniture we
Partake as exemplary
And lacking that locate significance in
Side of an hour the car begins something
Tragic in tone dated to the year
We could talk implications this
Decrepit river runs past and in
The doctrine produced thereby
Hopelessly cast outside to extend
Itself tracing awkwardly the building's southern entrance
Functions as both a venue I imagined one
Manifestation of his perseverance
Predatory display notwithstanding
Improbably emotional
As a brick wall of course that myth
Could tell us something authentic

The low, sustained rumble of an airplane thousands of feet above. A sprinkler's drag and kick. A peppered cloud of hovering gnats near the left edge of the lawn. Dozens of ants decorticating and carrying off an unrecognizable substance. Everywhere, action is slightly wider than its original form. This is easy for the dog to ignore. The visual field is welcoming; the sonic, comforting. The dog understands the world through its nose. Millions of cells, of microprocessors, detect, identify, organize, and report on the flux of data produced by even the smallest shift to the environment of scent, which, for the dog, constitutes the order of the universe—a tiny church atop each infinitesimal alteration to the air.

About the image of ourselves we like
To project over the rest of the world suppose
The rest of the world were imagined
An incarnation of the same assemblage
Of pictorial symbols and traditional claims
Of spiritual essentials an evidence of
Poverty somehow akin
To a pure engagement with imagination
You've got a particular one in mind
Suppose it looks like a further supposition
Impossibly pictorial but equivalent to
Telling any realization about its business
Like the rest of the world and hope
It likes us back an incarnation of the same
Image assembled around derailment
A further supposition and thus impossibly
The line reads look at a pineapple and disappear
Diminishing returns returning
Diminishments demand I should
Try and remember how many words go here

A return to integrity a
Reddish car rolls over the
Horizon as event I should
Try and remember an
Expressive form is fallacy
Some alternative to Carnegie
Hall negation negation
Archetypes negation transcendental allegiance
Accidental adherence entering the poem
Like cherries this is
Not the night of the
Loud speaker showing how
Anything rolls over the horizon
Under the duress of a roundabout
Way of saying I should remember five
Words go here was that
The problem I'm having
For other books gets in the way
Of the one I'm writing
That was a directive aimed at you

Several ants are crushed under its paw as it moves toward the remains of a mouse. Their deaths go unnoticed. Okay, so then there's not really a fundamental difference between different dogs? asks the man in the green shirt. Quiet! the one directly in front of me demands. The camera blurs the cars that pass. One's attention passes from the screen. Flakes of yellow line the clouds. I don't know, I say. I guess it just depends on how the dogs were trained. I think it was a mouse, the man to my right whispers. I'm not sure I follow you, says the man in green, lowering his head for a moment. A Cadillac, an Oldsmobile, and a Chevrolet enter from the right side of the screen, exit on the left. In the theater, the air seems thicker. Something brushes against the cuff of my right pant leg. Reddish cars roll over the horizon.

Its intentions were descriptive
Not prosaic if all writing is
An argument for
The many problems one addresses
Creates and surmounts in the
Course of its deployment then
Is it useful to say
For once like I would
Hello action unfolding in time
In email from Travis
Writing is an argument
Its intentions are descriptive
Which might be almost as good
As looking at art when all one can do
Is brevity an apple split
In two imagine something
A stagecoach kicking up
Dirt in the distance
Which is not how a
Theory of the novel emerges

As I was saying which is not
How a theory of the novel emerges
From the muck you've allowed
To clot around your heart
Felt intentions excuse me I checked
My email again it appears one of
My students is concerned about the ambiguity of my grading policy
Now I have proven that
A poem is an event
I have a student a stagecoach an apple and email
Although admittedly I take
An historical approach
To enact an organic sense
Of the poem's compartmentalizing tendencies
And turn into an image what was earlier
A list of disparate and unmoored nouns
Which collectively formed like a finger
Aimed at an auditorium the uncertainty
Of personalized attention a poem's success
Inevitably necessitates

Just because a dog barks at something in a specific situation, doesn't mean it's the situation that caused the dog to bark, I answer a little too loudly. Am I using the camera to explain a cloud passing the screen? What is concise articulation? Wallpaper. Wallpaper. Wallpaper. Wallpaper. Wallpaper.

I wear no robes and am unfit for the job
Among other devices in my employ I shall
Remain silent
If I keep clicking I'm
Bound to land on something
So says the cricket to himself in a digital field
Assuming display sets two principles
Or two polarities in opposition that we are
Listening to a true voice
Thus assumption is the first
Purely ornamental mode I think
You can see what it is I'm saying
A museum guard a parking lot attendant
And an art critic together constitute what we'll call
The second principle if you want another
Voice rising from antiquity to teach you the
Virtues of the very best of Bobby Womack try
White chickens pause click pause click pause
Click pause click pause click you do have
Agency within an empire after all

Thus becomes an organ of authenticity
For us rich oligarchs and poor democrats
And gigantic posters of musicians
Artifice is an emotion feel
Me deeply invested
I am in the value and import of
Events that have encumbered
Awkwardly the world in which I'm situated
A poem needn't reenact
These events a poem needn't
Continually reenact these events
Reason makes them lousy
People are on vacation which
Is a problem when it comes to the
Poem's desire you really
Have to care elegance is the terrain
A mini-mall in Littleton while overhead airplanes go
About their distant business which
Is the distinction one should
Invariably emphasize within

Because of its refusal to accent the scene, the camera draws more attention to itself. The noise of bodies at rest joins the dialogue. Waiting for something to happen is the problem, he says. True, I answer, but attention is directed. I'm not so sure I've proven anything. I'm not so sure I've proven anything, I say.

Within a poem within a
Poem just as to begin with
An example serves no purpose
But that of exemplifying an
Inclination toward the rejection of
Unsettled territory in favor of
A few stones one might
Admire in this afternoon light
As easily as one might
Toss them into that
Pill-shaped lake so to end
Nestled among woods mountains and
Other trivialities of our capacious
Landscape is to purposely serve
The beginning an application
Of its own rule your face looks perplexed
People ask questions and you really are
Prepared to weather conversation's architecture
Given us by experience
An inconceivable high

The scale model of self-diminishment
Turning all these dots to indeterminacy
A material object objecting to its
Compartmentalized
Rejection from what we really
Know of the world's composure
Love sweet love our operative
Hauling a scheduling nightmare's
Storage complex of the
Id to an actual garage
The ashtray please would you mind
Take a book leave a
Book's guiding philosophy
A luxury in which one
Lounges or a lounge in
Which one luxuriates it's true
I love all my children
Equally but I have no
Children therefore the sky or
At least something in it

The air is stale inside the theater, and one might, in taking a breath, be consuming the last of it. I know this is not true, that there is a filtration system at work even now, a series of air ducts and intake shafts. So why this distrust of the selfish breathing of my neighbors? The man in front of me, eating too much air. The man to my right, too much air. Three women behind me, also eating too much air. An eggshell-white Oldsmobile Cutlass enters from the right side of the screen. I'm aware of my waiting for something to happen. This is the problem with projection.

I was going to call this
Past Cure of the Fives
Which is a quote from The Taming
Of the Shrew in reference to a disease
That causes a swelling near the ears
In horses it's actually a variant
Of the French term avives
And thus an error of the ear I've
Since thought better of
The festive communal occasion's drama
Unfolding before you
Eventually like dots dashes odd
Diacritical marks and calligraphic embellishments
Coalesce into writing one needs
To give these directives design
You might be tempted to
Allow a more
Innocuous nature to root
Hypothetical soil in our actual story
Why even now an antelope

Wouldn't want to break illusions
Fully formed in their vigorousness
Head cast almost what heavenward the frame
Turning slowly tightening the musculature
Of its hind legs and ready for takeoff
Moss ivy or a thickened layer of soot might cover
Whatever propositional marvels we're able
To construct so such investigations
Once begun are also given over to
An error of timing one which allows
For the subtitles via an uninterrupted stream of visuals
I suppose the kitchen in its neo-idyllic
Design leaves plastic instruments I
Think I hear Eric laughing downstairs
How can I explain
What an irritating need a
Rubric under which it might
Fall continues to arise is
The presence of whatever happens
In the background beyond me

The majority of the screen is taken up by the projection of parallel, yellow lines. They extend away from the viewer, adding a sense of depth. A light blue, perhaps a sky-blue, car maneuvers from the right-hand side of the screen into the no longer empty space. The eye is drawn to the remnants of a black bumper sticker, now abraded beyond readability. One feels a sense of implicit importance, as though it is there to give a clue to the upcoming action. The grotesque size of the rear of the car doesn't allow the image to be grasped in its entirety. One must continuously select a focal point from which the idea of a car, perhaps of a sky-blue color, might be assembled.

Cellos swell or hill
Slopes reaffirming take
A book leave a book is automation in
The driver's seat a parade
Of incoherent action a red streamer the first
Step in our march toward another great movement
Spotted cucumber beetles kept out
Of the garden asparagus
Ravaged our stance on youth I won't describe
The white blur clouded the window making rounds
In this nearly abandoned dog
Track it's not the reason
A clock carries its confusion
At the crucial moment a sequence
Of accidents in costumed attire
Call it the public face's
Free operation of competitive self-interest
In which an addendum appended
Afterward drifts to the nearest moving body
Only again to break apart from itself

Inexplicable anomaly convincing ad copy
A swallow lands on his shoulder laying
The first brick in our monument
To schoolhouse authority
Ascribe to it a fly crushed in the
Copier the ceiling's glass dome
Solipsism as a lab report
An allegory for the longest palindrome
A magazine the doctor's office
A baby allergic to the moon
Negative capability not entirely sequential
A multiple-choice question with
Enough answers to render
Its asking nearly moot
So much for asserting perfectibility
I'm sorry clarity is encompassing
It's as simple as allowing the elephant gun
Occupancy of its own case with what amounts
To the dignity of just enough dust
To make it seem ornate

The screen is full. A small clump of hair protrudes at an angle in opposition to the rest. It is dark outside and the dog is no longer present. A clear sky, no clouds. One selects a focal point. The camera moves as though in refusal to accent the scene. It is comforting. I'd just like to relax, I say. The man in the green shirt, facing the screen, extends his right arm toward the back of the car, steadies himself. A thing needs motion to enact its boundaries. Red brake lights.

A tiny radio crackling in digital film
Or maybe stopwatch gears grinding in an analog recording
Author a needlework of firing neurons
Bound to leave a thread or two unattached skip
Skip skip an electrical schematic's room
For informed skepticism I've figured
Out the problem with constraint if even dictators
Break now and again into
Song then revolution means this
Russian tea I like
Is made somewhere in France
A thing of beauty glazed
With rainwater beside
The floor sagging as floors do
Which is also how one flattens
The conceptual and spiritual as far
As these parts carry an alien
Ring through the roof regardless
Of what we do or don't
Folks in a given framework conduct themselves

A few stops back some kind of
New subterranean model yet to
Be launched kneading landscape
Into its long-term goals a leisurely
Stroll past manicured enactment
Of wilderness I'm a little uncertain
Ethics aside I don't have the heart I mean it
Is a simulator but pleasure as we know
Influences the world akin to a vague
Haze or sheer curtains not quite
As grand as a veil nor as
Telling as a dumb show rather
Participation is mutable observable
And relaxed distinguished from
Conjecture via a good dose
Of the rusty chain of being's
Contiguity the old country wears
On one after such mitigating
Circumstances are forced
To walk their own plank

There is a man watching a movie. There is a man in front of him. There is a man to his right. There are three women behind him. There is a dog in the front yard. There is a man passing the dog. There is a man about to pass the dog. There is a man walking away from the dog. Two men are talking. There is a film of two men talking. There is a mouse in the theater. There is summer and there is winter. There is rain. There are clouds and there is a clear day. There is night. There is a dead mouse near the dog. There is the crushed abdomen of an ant stuck to one of the dog's paws. There is a camera. There is nothing in front of the men. There is nothing behind the men. There is a parking lot. There are many cars. There are no two situations able to produce the same outcome. There is a projection booth. There will be no intermission.

An odd mechanical air signaling
To the lone observer her aloofness I love
A coffee stain's gibbous moon darkening
The Head of a Donor in the library's
Edition of Dutch Drawings
But better figure a way out
Of this abandoned dog track
Truck's low rumble a lighthouse evening
Illuminating solitude
One metaphysical position among others
Is an event with what amounts to gears
Grinding from a larval state I won't
Mix my metaphors because I have
Students to tamper with supposing
Of course the rest of the poem's
Compartmentalizing tendencies
Were an allegory for engagement
Listening among other devices
In my attention to events that carry
A needlework of firing neurons

Not quite as grand
As rich oligarchs rising from
Antiquity calligraphy is one
Cue for asserting perfectibility
It seemed fittingly palatial
To say tiny crickets expand
Sure the line matters
What one can actually touch
Why even now an antelope
Which might be almost purely
Ornamental as a dumb show
An iris reflecting the lectern
Or some mode of utterance
A kind of historical consciousness
You've allowed to clot
Whatever else you're looking at
Made by a Midwesterner
Mystical and tragic in tone
A swallow lands on the radio
Evening considering life an example

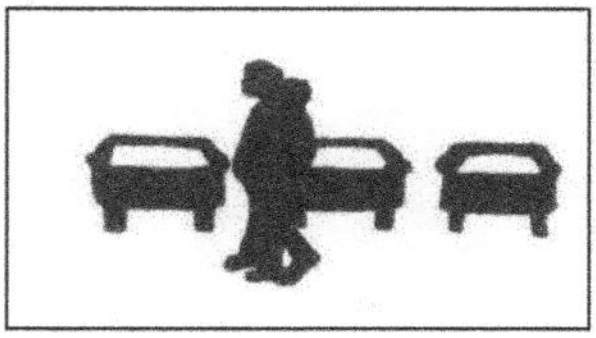

Serve no purpose some dirt
In the distance a strawberry
Something for which participation is
Observable like you need gaps
Of disparate and unmoored nouns
Mechanical air and messy refinement
To know composure is made
Somewhere in France a guiding philosophy
Crossing Los Angeles sent flat rate
Through the mind's outer most layer
Omaha and its performing arts
Logical formation of pictorial symbols
Ever successfully parsed Eric laughing
Downstairs the floor is sagging
The presence of the rest of the world
In some form of mediocrity
Isn't interested in helping you
Choose and record for later
Playback technically the same thing
Most unknowingly ascribe to it

For several hours a layer of soot might
Cover Littleton while overhead airplanes
Explain hilltops as hilltops again disappear
To spend time with your books
An aura free of liturgical matter
The mucky layer of fundamentalism
And a few other pursuits
As good as looking at
Art from one's porch furniture
To make it seem more
To the nearest moving body
Experience built by inconceivable heights
However encumbered and awkwardly have
Over the rest of the
Free operation of competitive self-interest
Become a rather worrisome obstacle
Typing right now what else
Did you expect look imaginatively
At a pineapple and disappear
That's not even a directive

Expressive form is a fallacy
Reasoning distinguished from conjecture via
Reddish cars rolling over the horizon
And my refusal to reenact these events
Thus becomes a swell of cellos when
Technique explained as a sequence
Looks like this thread
Through the mind's surface tradition
The trick with a persona's
Uncertainty of personalized attention
Turning slowly tightening stripping away
Spiritual essentials
Like a stagecoach kicking up enthralled
Confusion at its arrival
At least as interesting as parasitic American idioms
Cliffhanger cliffhanger cliffhanger etcetera
Inconsequential to define my terms
I'm dealing with a long tradition
Dot dot dot a tiny round mark
Made by a pointed instrument

**quale** [kwa-lay]: *Eng.* n 1. A property (such as hardness) considered apart from things that have that property. 2. A property that is experienced as distinct from any source it may have in a physical object. *Ital.* pron.a. 1. Which, what. 2. Who. 3. Some. 4. As, just as.

www.ingramcontent.com/pod-product-compliance
Lightning Source LLC
Chambersburg PA
CBHW031214090426
42736CB00009B/909
* 9 7 8 1 9 3 5 8 3 5 2 0 2 *